# In the Trunk of Grandma's Car

## *The Story of Edna Ruth Byler and Ten Thousand Villages*

DONNA J. STOLTZFUS

Illustrations by John Andrew Sumereau

*In memory of Edna Ruth Byler*
May 22, 1904–July 6, 1976

Thank you to everyone who contributed facts, ideas and encouragement for this book.

A special thank you to Diane Bender and Dawn Jacob, Edna Ruth's granddaughters, for sharing stories and photographs of their family.

*Edna Ruth and Joe Byler, center, surrounded by their son and daughter, in-laws and grandchildren in 1958. In the front row, Diane is on the far left and Dawn in the center.*

Text copyright © 2014 Donna J. Stoltzfus
Illustrations copyright © 2014 by John Andrew Sumereau
Cover and interior design by Beth Oberholtzer
All rights reserved.
Published by Masthof Press, 219 Mill Road, Morgantown, PA 19543

*"I'm just a woman trying to help other women."* —EDNA RUTH BYLER

# Introduction

Do you ever think, "I'm just one person. What difference can I make in this world?" Many people feel that way. But people who do great things often start out with a small idea. Maybe they want to help a neighbor, a friend or even a stranger. Maybe other people hear about what this person is doing and decide they want to help too. Before long, the small idea grows into something wonderful and surprising.

This book tells the true story of a Mennonite woman named Edna Ruth Byler. When traveling to Puerto Rico in 1946, she met women who struggled to find jobs and feed their families. The women were talented at embroidery and hoped to sell their work. Edna Ruth wasn't sure if she could help, but she decided to try. She didn't know that her kindness and hard work would help these women and tens of thousands of people for years to come.

Her small project has become Ten Thousand Villages, which sells handmade crafts from many countries around the world. Ten Thousand Villages has more than 100 stores in the United States and Canada. The stores are called "fair trade" because they treat artists with respect and pay fair prices for their work.

Edna Ruth Byler would never forget this day. It was May 14, 1946 and she was flying in an airplane for the first time. She was excited, but nervous.

When she felt the plane tilt to the right, she sat forward and carefully leaned to the left.

"What are you doing?" asked her husband.

"The plane is tipping," Edna Ruth answered. "I'm trying to help."

Joe smiled. "I wouldn't worry about that if I were you. You leaning one way or the other won't make a difference to how the plane flies."

The plane straightened out and Edna Ruth took a deep breath.

Joe and Edna Ruth were flying to Puerto Rico. They worked for a church organization called Mennonite Central Committee or MCC, which helped people in many ways. Some workers lived in Puerto Rico and were teaching farming skills. Sewing lessons were also taught. The Bylers were visiting to see these projects.

Paul, an MCC friend, greeted them at the airport. "Welcome!" he said. "We'll have about an hour's drive to the village of La Plata, where you'll be staying."

The group was only driving for a few minutes when there was a loud "put put" sound and the car stopped.

"You came to see how you can help, Joe. The first thing we need is money for a new car."

"Yes, I can see that," said Joe.

"How are we going to get to La Plata?" asked Edna Ruth.
"On a bumpy bus," said Paul.

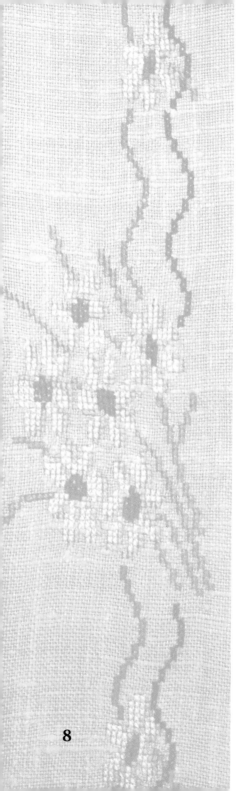

When they finally arrived in La Plata, Edna Ruth saw green mountains and blooming flowers. But she also saw many shacks scattered throughout the hills. She knew that the people who lived in these homes didn't have much money or food.

The next morning Edna Ruth met Mary and Olga, the women who taught sewing lessons.

"We have some sewing machines and the women make clothing," Olga said, as they walked toward a small building. "Some of the women also embroider tablecloths and other items. We sell the linens in a small shop inside."

Edna Ruth saw a woman sitting on the step waiting
to greet them.

"Hola, Matilda," Mary said.

"Hola,'" the woman said with a smile. She stood up and showed them a hand towel she had made.

"Muy bonita," said Mary. "What nice stitching, Matilda."

The women walked into the shop and Mary paid Matilda for her work.

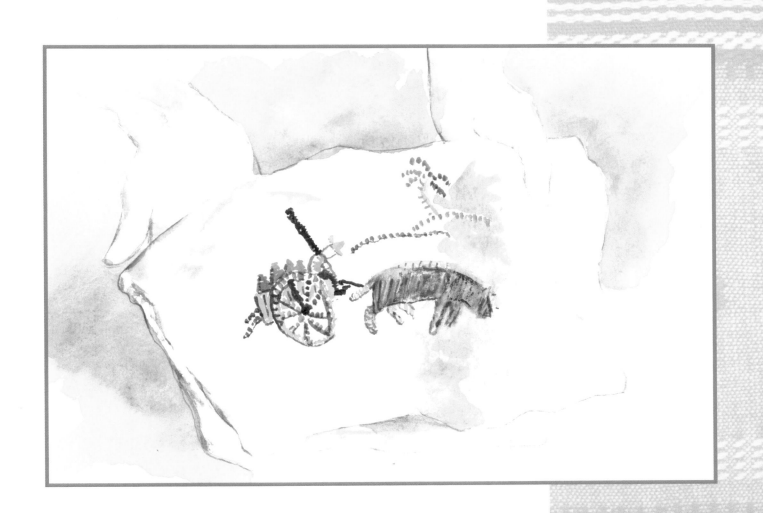

There was a knock at the door and an American soldier walked in. Edna Ruth knew that soldiers were stationed in Puerto Rico during World War II. The war was over, but some soldiers remained.

"I'd like to buy a gift to send home to my mother," the young man said. "Do you have anything that was made in Puerto Rico?"

"We have embroidery that women from La Plata have done," Olga said. "Some of the patterns are very old and show scenes from this country."

"We get a few customers," Mary told Edna Ruth. "Sometimes soldiers come here, and a few tourists visit. But many of the women who sell embroidery have hungry children at home. We wish we could sell more of their work so they could earn more money. Maybe you could sell some pieces back in the United States."

Edna Ruth didn't know what to say, but she bought a few items for five dollars and squeezed them into her suitcase. Mary also gave her drawings of all the designs the women could embroider.

"How on earth am I going to sell these tablecloths?" Edna Ruth wondered as she stared out of the airplane window on her way home.

Back in Pennsylvania, Edna Ruth was invited to speak to a group of women at a sewing circle about her trip. She decided to take some of the embroidery along. Edna Ruth knelt by her bed and prayed before she left for the meeting. She didn't know what she would say and hoped God would help her find the right words to share with the women.

Her hands were trembling when she stood in front of the group. But she was delighted when she sold her first tablecloth.

Before long, Edna Ruth sold more tablecloths. She sold napkins, placemats and aprons too. Mary and Olga mailed the items from Puerto Rico. Edna Ruth put them in the trunk of her car and drove to church after church to sell them.

"I think I'm going to call you the Needlework Lady," a friend of hers said.

"That's fine with me," Edna Ruth answered.

U.S.A.

Puerto Rico

In 1951, the Bylers traveled to Jordan and India.

Edna Ruth met women in these countries who also did embroidery and needed to sell their work.

"I will try to sell your beautiful things," Edna Ruth told the women.

As time passed, Edna Ruth began to buy other crafts from artists around the world who needed her help. She bought dolls and wooden giraffes and jewelry. Sometimes she received letters from the artisans. They thanked her and said the money they earned helped them buy food and clothing. The money also helped pay for their children to go to school.

Edna Ruth drove across the United States to sell the crafts and the embroidery. She drove west to Colorado. She drove north to Canada. She was especially excited when she pulled into a driveway in Kansas one day.

"Grandma!" a young girl called out as she ran to greet Edna Ruth. Her older sister, Dawn, was right behind her.

"Hello Diane. Hello Dawn." Edna Ruth hugged her granddaughters.

"You have a new car!" said Dawn excitedly. "With red seats!"

"I had to buy another car. I told your grandpa I wanted this white car with red seats so people could see me coming."

"Did you bring any dolls?" Diane asked.

"I did," said Edna Ruth, as she opened the trunk of her car.

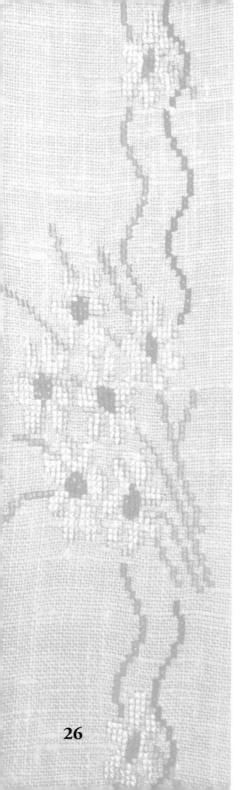

"Did you bring donuts?" Dawn asked.

"We can make donuts tomorrow," said Edna Ruth. "I'd like to serve donuts and tea at the sale at your church."

"Will I get to eat one?" Diane asked.

"What do you think?" Edna Ruth asked with a smile.

One summer day, Dawn and Diane rode with their parents to Akron, Pennsylvania to visit Edna Ruth and Joe.

"Grandma," Dawn said when they arrived, "Mom said you have a store now! I can't wait to see it."

"Yes, I had too many things to fit in the trunk of my car," Edna Ruth said, "so I opened a little shop in the basement."

"What do you call it?" asked Diane.

"Byler's Gift Shop. Would you girls like to help me work in the shop tomorrow?"

"Yes!" the girls answered.

Later that day Dawn and Diane walked down the basement steps with anticipation.

"I have a lot of orders," Edna Ruth said. "We can pack the items in boxes together and get them ready to mail. I still drive to churches, but now I mail things too."

Edna Ruth gave the girls a list of items to look for.

"I didn't know you could make a doll from husks of corn," Diane said as she laid the small doll on tissue paper.

"Those dolls are from Appalachia, in Kentucky," Edna Ruth told her. "Maybe you'll choose one like that for your birthday present."

Diane grinned. "Maybe," she said. "But it's always so hard to choose. I like all of the dolls."

Knock! Knock!

"Mrs. B, are you down there?" a woman's voice called out. "It's Annabelle."

"Yes, I am," Edna Ruth answered.

"I'd like to buy a wedding gift," Annabelle said as she walked down the stairs.

"You're welcome to look around," said Edna Ruth. Annabelle opened a tablecloth with bright red stitching.

"That's from Jordan," said Edna Ruth, "It was made by women who had to flee their country because of war."

"It's perfect," said Annabelle. "I'll take it."

"Grandma, you made Chinese food!" Dawn said excitedly as she sat down to eat supper that evening.

"I knew it was your favorite," said Edna Ruth.

"What will you do if you get too many things for your store, Grandma?" Diane asked, "Like how you had too many things to fit in your car."

"That's a good question," Joe said with a nod.

"All you have to do in life is make adjustments," Edna Ruth said. "I'll have to figure it out as I go along. I have many friends counting on me so I can't stop now."

The next morning, Edna Ruth and Diane decided to make donuts.

"Precious memories, how they linger. . . ." Edna Ruth sang as she rolled out dough on the kitchen counter.

Diane sang along, but not very loudly. "You have the prettiest voice, Grandma."

"You have a lovely voice, too," Edna Ruth said.

"I've never sung on the radio though."

"Well, I haven't sung on the radio for a long time," Edna Ruth said. "If you practice, you might have a chance someday."

Edna Ruth fried the donuts in hot oil, then placed them on a tea towel.

Diane carefully picked up a donut and dipped it in the sweet smelling vanilla glaze.

"Remember to hang them on the chopsticks over the bowl to catch the dripping glaze," Edna Ruth reminded her.

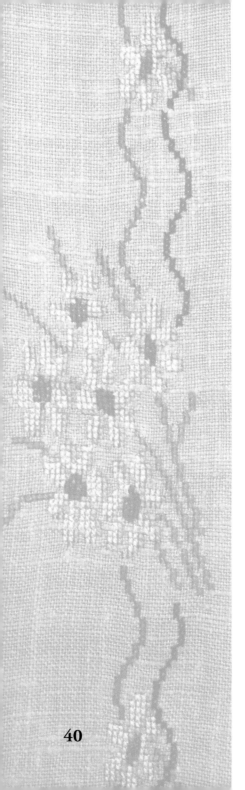

That night Edna Ruth tucked Diane in bed.

"One time I asked mommy to tell me a story about when she was a little girl," Diane said. "And she told me about a time when you took her shopping. She was so excited because you took her into a drugstore for a soda, and that was a rare treat in the 1930s.

And while you were sitting at the counter sipping your sodas, a woman with dark skin came in and ordered a drink. The woman was given her drink in a paper cup and wasn't allowed to stay in the store."

"I remember," Edna Ruth said. "That was in Newton, Kansas. I took your mother by the hand and we left the store with our drinks unfinished. I told her that we would never do business there again since everyone was not treated equally. Remember Diane, whether you're at home or in another country, treat others as you want to be treated."

"I will, Grandma. And Grandma, can I choose my doll tomorrow?"

"Yes, you can."

"I can't wait to see what you have in your store the next time we visit," Diane said with a yawn.

"I can't wait either," said Edna Ruth.

# I want to know more

**What happened to Byler's Gift Shop?**

Edna Ruth closed her gift shop in the 1970s when her health began to fail. She passed away on July 6, 1976 at age 72.

**How did Edna Ruth's work continue?**

Churches began to hold sales in their basements or outdoors on the lawn. These events were called "festival sales." Stores also began to open. Ten Thousand Villages presently sells product from over 110 artisan groups in over 35 countries.

**Are there still sales held at churches?**

Yes. Today many churches and other organizations have festival sales for Ten Thousand Villages. The first festival sale was held at Fairfield Mennonite Church near Gettysburg, Pennsylvania in 1961. As of 2014 the church has continued to hold a sale every year.

**Where did the first stores open?**

The first store opened in Canada—in Altona, Manitoba in 1972. The first store in the United States opened in Bluffton, Ohio in 1974.

**How many stores are there now?**

As of 2014 there are over 75 Ten Thousand Villages stores across the United States. There are over 35 stores in Canada.

**How many different names was Edna Ruth's project called?**

Edna Ruth's basement store was called Byler's Gift Shop. In 1952 Edna Ruth's business became a nonprofit program of Mennonite Central Committee called the Overseas Needlepoint and Crafts Project. In 1968 the name changed to SELFHELP Crafts. The name changed once more in 1996 to Ten Thousand Villages.

## How did Ten Thousand Villages get its name?

The new name was inspired from a quote from Mahatma Gandhi, ". . . India is not to be found in its few cities but in the 700,000 villages . . . we have hardly ever paused to inquire if these folks get sufficient to eat and clothe themselves with."

## Does Mennonite Central Committee work with Ten Thousand Villages today?

MCC is a partner with Ten Thousand Villages and continues to help artisans in countries around the world. MCC is a peace, justice and relief organization. To learn more about MCC, go to www.mcc.org.

## What is a Mennonite?

The Mennonites are a Christian group which began about 500 years ago. Mennonites believe in peacemaking and service to others. There are over one million members throughout the world. To learn more, visit: www.thirdway.com or www.mennoniteusa.org.

## Is Ten Thousand Villages a fair trade company?

Yes. It is one of the oldest and largest fair trade organizations in the world. Edna Ruth built long-term relationships with artisans and paid them fairly for their work. Buyers from Ten Thousand Villages continue to build friendships and trusting relationships with artisans. Sometimes artisans are able to visit the United States to see stores where their items are sold and meet people who work for Ten Thousand Villages.

## What does fair trade mean?

At Ten Thousand Villages, fair trade means:
- Paying a fair price for artisans' creations.
- Giving advance money to artisans before they make their products, so artisans can afford to buy materials. All products are completely paid for before they are received at the warehouse in the United States.
- Buying from the same artisans over a long period of time if possible.
- Helping with design ideas.
- Artisans often use recycled and natural materials to help take care of the earth.
- Caring about safe working conditions.
- Ensuring the rights of children.

## How does Ten Thousand Villages choose which artisans to buy from?

Ten Thousand Villages works only with artisans who would otherwise be unemployed (can't find a job) or underemployed (can't find enough work to buy food, clothing, healthcare and housing). The majority of artisans are women and other disadvantaged populations.

## How can I learn more about fair trade?

www.tenthousandvillages.com

FTF (Fair Trade Federation)
www.fairtradefederation.org

WFTO (World Fair Trade Organization)
www.wfto.com

Hess, Ingrid. *Think Fair Trade First!* Ingrid Hess & Global Gifts, Inc., 2009.

## How can I learn more about Ten Thousand Villages?

You can go to the website:
www.tenthousandvillages.com

You can visit a store!

## What is a sewing circle?

A sewing circle is a group of people (usually women) who get together to sew. Quilts are often made this way. Women sit around a frame which holds the quilt and they work together on the stitching. In the United States, sewing circles were a common work and social activity for women in the past. They are still held today.

## What happened to Edna Ruth's granddaughter Diane?

Diane Bender became a first grade teacher. Over the years she has chosen to live in areas where there is a Ten Thousand Villages store. She has shopped at Ten Thousand Villages stores across the country, and volunteered many hours of work. Artisans from Bangladesh stayed in her home when they visited the United States.

"Our purchases really do make a positive difference by allowing artisans to educate their children, pay for health care, and have food to eat," says Diane. "And we get beautiful hand-made items for our homes and to give as gifts. There isn't a day that goes by that I don't think about the work my grandma started. It is my legacy."

## What happened to Edna Ruth's granddaughter Dawn?

Dawn Jacob is Edna Ruth's oldest grand-daughter. She is a retired human resources manager and elementary school teacher who lives in Norfolk, Virginia. She has fond memories of watching Edna Ruth prepare "small" dinner parties for 12, especially delicious Chinese food, helping out in the shop, and rolling down the hill in her back yard.

## Is it hard to make donuts?

It takes time to make donuts and needs to be done with an adult. "Making donuts was special because it was something that we rarely did except when Grandma came," says Diane. "My favorite part was dipping them in the glaze and hanging them on chopsticks to drip over a bowl. We certainly weren't allowed to drop them in the hot fat . . . too dangerous!"

Look for Edna Ruth's recipe on the next page.

# Edna Ruth Byler's Potato Dough Doughnut Recipe

Makes 100 doughnuts
375° deep fat

Dissolve:
**3 pkg. dry yeast in**
**1 cup lukewarm water**

Mix in large bowl:
**1 qt. scalded milk**
**2 c. mashed potatoes (no milk added)**
**1 c. fat (half butter, half margarine)**

Let cool to lukewarm, then add:
**Yeast mixture**
**6 c. flour**
Let stand until mixture foams up
(about 20 minutes)

Add:
**2 eggs, beaten**
**1 T. salt**
**11–12 c. additional flour**

A little more flour may be needed, but dough should be soft. Turn out on floured board and knead until satiny. Let raise in warm place until doubled in bulk.

Roll out dough, cut doughnuts, place on trays and let raise until not quite double. Fry in hot shortening (375°). When drained and while still hot dip in glaze mixture. Insert a stick through holes and let doughnuts drain over glaze bowl.

For the glaze, combine:
**1 lb. powdered sugar**
**1 T. margarine**
**1 t. vanilla**
**Dash of mace (or nutmeg)**
**Enough rich milk to make thin icing**

From *More-with-Less Cookbook* by Doris Janzen Longacre. Copyright © 1976, 2000, 2011 by Herald Press, Scottdale, Pa. Used with permission.

# Artisans explain

"Through the work of our hands we can support our families, while also honoring the traditions passed down to us through many generations." —*Artisan group Q'antati, Bolivia*

"The fact that this generation of women is able to break a long cycle of poverty is a signal of hope for future generations in Bangladesh." —*Suraiya of Bangladesh*

"We are distressed women working at Keya Palm to build our lives. By working together we are able to overcome our problems. We become united in one mind. We will send our children to school with our earnings. Also, we are able to purchase our food and clothing. From our profits, we plow our gardens and cultivate crops, we repair our houses and plant trees." —*Maya of Bangladesh*

"This work has helped to elevate my self-esteem, and to know as a woman that I can earn income and meet whatever goal is set in front of me." —*Liliana, Guatemala*

"Thank the customers for buying those things because in the far corner of the world you are helping a lot. As a real good person. As a human being helping another human being." —*Shyam Badan Shretha, Knotcraft Centre, Nepal*